Home-Tested Casserole Recipes

Publications International, Ltd.

Favorite Brand Name Recipes at www.fbnr.com

Favorite Brand Name is a trademark of Publications International, Ltd.

Front cover photography and photography on pages 15, 17, 23, 27, 37, 41, 45, 65, 73, 77, 83 and 89 by Stephen Hamilton Photographics, Inc., Chicago
Photographers: Stephen Hamilton, Tate Hunt
Photographers' Assistant: Jed Leland
Food Stylists: Donna Coats, Josephine Orba, Susie Skoog
Assistant Food Stylist: Carol Radford

Photography on back cover and pages 7, 9, 11, 19, 30, 33, 47, 51, 55, 59, 63, 69, 75, 79, 85 and 87 by Proffitt Photography, Ltd., Chicago
Photographer: Laurie Proffitt
Photographer's Assistant: Chad Evans
Food Stylist: Carol Smoler
Assistant Food Stylist: Liza Brown
Prop Stylist: Paula Walters

Pictured on the front cover: Zucornchile Rajas Bake *(page 44),* submitted by Elaine Sweet (inset photo).

Pictured on the back cover *(from top to bottom):* Cha-Cha-Cha Casserole *(page 32)* and Baked Risotto with Asparagus, Spinach and Parmesan *(page 50)***.**

ISBN: 0-7853-9293-9

Manufactured in U.S.A.

8 7 6 5 4 3 2 1

Microwave Cooking: Microwave ovens vary in wattage. Use the cooking times as guidelines and check for doneness before adding more time.

CONTENTS

GREAT GROUND MEAT

 ## Pizza Casserole

Richard White ◆ Lewistown, PA

    2 cups uncooked rotini or other spiral pasta
1½ to 2 pounds ground beef
    1 medium onion, chopped
        Salt and pepper
    1 can (about 15 ounces) pizza sauce
    1 can (8 ounces) tomato sauce
    1 can (6 ounces) tomato paste
    ½ teaspoon sugar
    ½ teaspoon garlic salt
    ½ teaspoon dried oregano leaves
    2 cups (8 ounces) shredded mozzarella cheese
12 to 15 slices pepperoni

1. Preheat oven to 350°F. Cook rotini according to package directions. Set aside.

2. Meanwhile, cook and stir ground beef and onion in large skillet over medium-high heat until meat is no longer pink. Season with salt and pepper. Set aside.

3. Combine rotini, pizza sauce, tomato sauce, tomato paste, sugar, garlic salt and oregano in large bowl. Add beef mixture and combine.

4. Place half of mixture in 3-quart casserole and top with 1 cup cheese. Repeat layers. Arrange pepperoni slices on top. Bake 25 to 30 minutes or until heated through and cheese melts.

Makes 6 to 8 servings

Meat Crust Pie

Chris Gelinskey ◆ Oconomowoc, WI

1 pound ground beef
2 cans (8 ounces each) tomato sauce, divided
½ cup seasoned dry bread crumbs
¼ cup minced onion
½ cup chopped green bell pepper, divided
1 teaspoon salt, divided
⅛ teaspoon dried oregano leaves
⅛ teaspoon pepper
1 cup water
1⅓ cups instant rice
1 cup grated Cheddar cheese, divided

1. Preheat oven to 350°F. Combine beef, ½ cup tomato sauce, bread crumbs, onion, ¼ cup bell pepper, ½ teaspoon salt, oregano and pepper in large bowl; mix well. Pat onto bottom and side of ungreased 9-inch, deep-dish pie plate.

2. Bring water and remaining ½ teaspoon salt to boil in medium saucepan. Stir in rice; cover and remove from heat. Let stand 5 minutes or until water is absorbed. Add remaining 1½ cups tomato sauce, ½ cup cheese and remaining ¼ cup bell pepper to rice and combine. Spoon rice mixture into meat shell. Cover with foil and bake 25 minutes.

3. Remove from oven and drain fat carefully, holding a pan lid in place to keep pie from sliding. Top with remaining ½ cup cheese and return to oven. Bake uncovered 10 to 15 minutes or until cheese melts. Carefully drain fat again. Cut into wedges to serve.

Makes 6 to 8 servings

Spicy Beefy Noodles

Marlene Roberts ◆ *Moore, OK*

1½ pounds ground beef
1 small onion, minced
1 small clove garlic, minced
1 tablespoon chili powder
1 teaspoon paprika
⅛ teaspoon *each* of dried basil, dill weed, thyme and marjoram
    Salt and pepper
1 can (10 ounces) diced tomatoes with green chilies, undrained
1 can (8 ounces) tomato sauce
1 cup water
3 tablespoons Worcestershire sauce
1 package (about 10 ounces) noodles, cooked according to package directions
½ cup *each* shredded Cheddar, mozzarella, pepper jack and provolone cheeses

1. Cook and stir ground beef with onion and garlic in large skillet over medium heat until meat is no longer pink; drain well. Add chili powder, paprika, basil, dill, thyme and marjoram. Season with salt and pepper. Cook and stir 2 minutes.

2. Add diced tomatoes, tomato sauce, water and Worcestershire sauce. Mix well and simmer, covered, 20 minutes.

2. In microwave-safe, 2-quart casserole combine meat sauce and noodles. Mix shredded cheeses and sprinkle evenly over top.

3. Microwave at HIGH 3 minutes. Let stand 5 minutes. Microwave 3 minutes longer or until cheeses melt.

Makes 6 servings

Home Cook's Hint

When buying ground beef it helps to know that USDA standards require all ground beef to be at least 70 percent lean. Ground sirloin and ground round are leaner. When looking for the best price on ground beef, keep in mind that leaner cuts cost more per pound, but produce less fat to drain off.

Zucchini Parmigiana Casserole

Tanya Bates ◆ Clearwater, FL

2 cups Italian-seasoned bread crumbs
½ cup flour
3 eggs, beaten
6 cups sliced zucchini
½ cup olive oil
1 pound lean ground beef
½ pound sausage
1 cup chopped onion
1 tablespoon minced garlic
¼ cup chopped fresh basil
2 tablespoons chopped fresh oregano
4 cups tomato sauce
2 cups (8 ounces) shredded mozzarella
¼ cup grated Parmesan cheese
4 tablespoons chopped fresh parsley

1. Preheat oven to 350°F. Place bread crumbs, flour and eggs in separate shallow bowls. Dip zucchini in flour, egg, then bread crumbs to coat. Heat olive oil in medium skillet over medium-high heat. Brown zucchini on both sides in batches; season with salt and pepper. Drain zucchini on paper towels. Drain fat from skillet.

2. Add ground beef, sausage, onion and garlic to skillet. Cook and stir until meat is no longer pink. Drain fat. Stir in basil and oregano.

3. Layer half of tomato sauce, half of zucchini, half of meat mixture, half of mozzarella and half of Parmesan in 4-quart casserole. Repeat layers.

4. Bake 30 minutes or until heated through and cheese is melted. Top with parsley.

Makes 6 servings

Oven-Baked Black Bean Chili

Carolyn Blakemore ◆ *Fairmont, WV*

1½ pounds lean ground beef
¼ cup chopped sweet onion
¼ cup chopped green bell pepper
1 can (about 15 ounces) black beans, rinsed and drained
1 can (14½ ounces) diced tomatoes with green chilies
1 can (about 14 ounces) beef broth
1 can (8 ounces) tomato sauce
5 tablespoons chili powder
1 tablespoon sugar
1 tablespoon ground cumin
1 teaspoon dried minced onion
⅛ teaspoon garlic powder
⅛ teaspoon ground ginger
2 cups (8 ounces) Mexican-blend shredded cheese

1. Preheat oven to 350°F. Cook and stir beef, onion and bell pepper in large skillet over medium-high heat until meat is no longer pink. Drain and transfer to 4-quart casserole.

2. Add remaining ingredients, except cheese, and stir to combine. Cover and bake 30 minutes, stirring every 10 minutes or so. Uncover, top with cheese, and return to oven for 5 minutes or until cheese melts.

Makes 6 to 8 servings

Carolyn says: This chili is great served with Mexican-style cornbread!

Old-Fashioned Cabbage Rolls

Arnita Jones ◆ McKenzie, TN

½ pound ground beef
½ pound ground veal
½ pound ground pork
1 small onion, chopped
2 eggs, lightly beaten
½ cup dry bread crumbs
1 teaspoon salt
1 teaspoon molasses
¼ teaspoon *each* ground ginger, ground nutmeg and ground allspice
1 large head cabbage, separated into leaves
3 cups boiling water
¼ cup butter or margarine
½ cup milk, or more as needed
1 tablespoon cornstarch

1. Mix meats and onion in large bowl. Combine eggs, bread crumbs, salt, molasses, ginger, nutmeg and allspice in medium bowl; add to meat mixture and combine well.

2. Drop cabbage leaves into boiling water for 3 minutes. Remove with slotted spoon, reserving ½ cup of boiling liquid.

3. Preheat oven to 375°F. Place 2 tablespoons of meat mixture 1 inch from stem end of each leaf. Fold sides in and roll up, fastening with toothpicks, if necessary.

4. Heat butter in large skillet over medium-high heat. Add cabbage rolls (3 or 4 at a time) to skillet and brown on all sides. Arrange rolls, seam-side down in a single layer in casserole. Combine reserved liquid with butter remaining in skillet and pour over cabbage rolls.

5. Bake 1 hour. Remove and drain accumulated pan juices into measuring cup. Add enough milk to pan juices to equal one cup.

6. Pour milk mixture into small saucepan, stir in cornstarch and bring to a boil, stirring constantly until sauce is thickened. Pour over cabbage rolls and bake 15 minutes more or until sauce is browned and cabbage is very tender.

Makes 8 servings

Athens Casserole

Barbara J. Dickinson ◆ *Harbor City, NJ*

2 tablespoons vegetable oil

1½ pounds eggplant, peeled, cut crosswise into ¼-inch slices

1½ pounds ground beef

2 cups chopped onions

1 medium green bell pepper, cut into strips

1 medium yellow bell pepper, cut into strips

1 medium red bell pepper, cut into strips

¼ cup red wine

4 tablespoons chopped parsley

1 teaspoon garlic powder

1 teaspoon ground cinnamon

Salt and pepper

2 cans (28 ounces each) stewed tomatoes

8 ounces feta cheese, crumbled

4 eggs, beaten

½ cup bread crumbs

1. Preheat oven to 350°F.

2. Heat oil in large skillet over medium-high heat. Add eggplant and brown on both sides, 5 to 7 minutes; set aside on paper towels to drain.

3. In same skillet, cook and stir ground beef, onions and bell peppers over medium heat until onion is transparent and beef is browned. Add wine, parsley, garlic powder and cinnamon; mix well. Season with salt and pepper.

4. Pour ⅓ of tomatoes into 13×9-inch baking dish. Add ⅓ of eggplant, ⅓ of beef mixture and ⅓ of cheese. Repeat layers until all ingredients are used. Pour eggs on top and sprinkle with bread crumbs.

5. Bake 45 minutes or until heated through and bubbly.

Makes 10 servings

CLASSIC COMBINATIONS

Delicious Ham & Cheese Puff Pie

Roxanne Chan ◆ Albany, CA

2 cups (about 1 pound) diced cooked ham
1 package (10 ounces) frozen chopped spinach, thawed and squeezed dry
½ cup diced red bell pepper
4 green onions, sliced
¾ cup all-purpose flour
¾ cup (3 ounces) shredded Swiss cheese
¾ cup milk
3 eggs
1 tablespoon prepared mustard
1 teaspoon grated lemon peel
1 teaspoon dried dill weed
½ teaspoon garlic salt
½ teaspoon ground black pepper
   Dill sprigs and lemon slices (optional)

1. Preheat oven to 425°F. Grease 2-quart casserole.

2. Combine ham, spinach, pepper and onions in prepared casserole.

3. Whisk together all remaining ingredients, except dill and lemon, in medium bowl; pour over ham mixture.

4. Bake 30 to 35 minutes or until puffed and browned. Cut into wedges and garnish with dill sprigs and lemon slices, if desired.

Makes 4 to 6 servings

Chicken Broccoli Rice Casserole

Shelley Hill ◆ Milwaukie, OR

3 cups cooked long grain rice

4 boneless skinless chicken breasts (about 1 pound), cooked and cut into bite-size pieces

1½ pounds broccoli, steamed until tender and cut into bite-size pieces

2 cans (10¾ ounces each) condensed cream of celery soup, undiluted

¾ cup mayonnaise

½ cup whole milk

2 teaspoons curry powder

3 cups (12 ounces) shredded sharp Cheddar cheese

1. Preheat oven to 350°F.

2. Butter 13×9-inch casserole. Place cooked rice evenly into casserole. Arrange chicken and broccoli on top. Mix together soup, mayonnaise, milk and curry powder in medium bowl; pour over chicken and broccoli. Top with cheese.

3. Cover loosely with foil and bake 45 minutes or until cheese melts and casserole is heated through.

Makes 4 to 6 servings

My Mac & Cheese

Carrie A. Theroux ◆ *Saco, ME*

4 tablespoons butter
4 tablespoons flour
2 cups milk
½ pound sharp Cheddar cheese, cut into ½-inch cubes
8 slices (about 4 ounces) pepper jack cheese (optional)
½ cup chopped onion
2 cups (about 16 ounces) broccoli florets, steamed until tender
2 cups macaroni, cooked and drained
2 English muffins, chopped into ½-inch pieces

1. Preheat oven to 350°F.

2. Melt butter in large saucepan over medium heat. Stir in flour to make a smooth paste; cook and stir 2 minutes. Gradually add milk, stirring contantly.

3. Add Cheddar cheese, pepper jack cheese, if desired, and onion to the milk mixture. Cook, stirring constantly, until cheese melts.

4. Add broccoli; stir well.

5. Place macaroni in 3-quart casserole. Add cheese and broccoli mixture; mix well. Sprinkle English muffin pieces evenly over top. Bake 15 to 20 minutes or until muffin pieces are golden brown.

Makes 4 to 6 servings

Lemon Shrimp

Aimee Dillman ◆ Midlothian, IL

1 package (12 ounces) egg noodles
½ cup (1 stick) butter
2 pounds cooked shrimp
3 tomatoes, chopped
1 cup chicken broth
1 cup shredded carrots
1 can (about 4 ounces) sliced mushrooms, drained
2 tablespoons fresh lemon juice
2 cloves garlic, chopped
½ teaspoon celery seed
¼ teaspoon black pepper

1. Preheat oven to 350°F.

2. Cook noodles according to package directions. Drain and mix with butter, stirring until butter is melted and noodles are evenly coated. Add remaining ingredients and mix again. Transfer to 3-quart casserole.

3. Bake 15 to 20 minutes or until heated through.

Makes 8 servings

Home Cook's Hint

Room temperature lemons will yield more juice than those right out of the refrigerator. Roll lemons back and forth on a hard surface applying downward pressure with your hand to break up the pulp and make them easier to juice. If you need to juice cold lemons, use the microwave to warm them. Microwave at HIGH for 20 seconds. One medium lemon yields about 3 tablespoons of juice.

Hawaiian Pork Chops

Brenda Imler ◆ Reddick, FL

 1 can (20 ounces) crushed pineapple, undrained
 2 large sweet potatoes, peeled and sliced
 1 teaspoon cinnamon
 6 to 8 boneless pork chops
 ½ teaspoon salt
 ½ teaspoon pepper

1. Preheat oven to 350°F. Grease 13×9-inch casserole.

2. Place crushed pineapple in casserole. Layer sweet potatoes over pineapple and sprinkle with cinnamon. Place pork chops on top and sprinkle with salt and pepper.

3. Cover with foil and bake about 1 hour or until sweet potatoes are tender and pork chops are tender and barely pink in center. Remove from oven. Increase oven temperature to 400°F. Remove foil and return casserole to oven. Bake about 10 minutes until liquid is reduced and chops are browned.

Makes 6 to 8 servings

Chicken Noodle Casserole

Alicia Freed ◆ Apple Valley, CA

 1 package (12 ounces) wide egg noodles
 1 can (10¾ ounces) condensed cream of mushroom soup, undiluted
 1 can (10¾ ounces) condensed cream of chicken soup, undiluted
 1 can (6 ounces) cooked white chicken
 ½ cup milk
 ½ cup shredded Cheddar Jack cheese
 ½ cup sour cream
 1 cup dry bread crumbs

1. Prepare egg noodles as directed on package. Drain well then place in large saucepan.

2. Add soups, chicken, milk, cheese and sour cream.

3. Cook and stir over medium heat until heated through.

4. Pour into 13×9-inch casserole and top with bread crumbs.

5. Place casserole under broiler for 5 to 10 minutes or until crispy on top.

Make 4 to 6 servings

Broccoli Chicken Cheese Fries Casserole

Maria L. Weiss ◆ *Somerset, MA*

3 tablespoons vegetable oil
5 boneless chicken breasts (about 1½ pounds), cut into bite-size pieces
½ package (about 8 ounces) frozen potato nuggets
1 package (10 ounces) frozen broccoli, thawed
2 cans (10¾ ounces each) condensed cheese soup, undiluted
1 cup bread crumbs
2 tablespoons butter or margarine, melted

1. Preheat oven to 400°F. Grease 3½-quart casserole.

2. Heat oil in large skillet over medium-high heat; add chicken. Cook and stir 5 to 10 minutes until chicken is no longer pink; drain.

3. Meanwhile, bake potato nuggets on *ungreased* baking sheet for 10 minutes; remove from oven. *Reduce oven temperature to 350°F.*

4. Combine chicken, potato nuggets, broccoli and 1 can of cheese soup in large bowl. Pour mixture into prepared casserole and add remaining can of soup. Combine bread crumbs and melted butter in small bowl; sprinkle over top.

5. Bake at 350°F 20 minutes or until browned and bubbly.

Makes 6 to 8 servings

4 Cheese Mac & Cheese

Beth Shaw ◆ *Pawcatuck, CT*

 1 package (16 ounces) uncooked macaroni
 4 cups milk
16 ounces sharp white Cheddar cheese, shredded
16 ounces American cheese, shredded
 8 ounces Muenster cheese, shredded
 8 ounces mozzarella cheese, shredded
 ½ cup bread crumbs

1. Cook macaroni according to package directions. Drain; set aside and keep warm.

2. In a large saucepan over medium heat, heat milk to almost boiling. *Reduce heat to low;* gradually add cheeses, stirring constantly. Cook and stir until all cheese has melted (about 5 minutes).

3. Place macaroni in 4-quart casserole. Pour cheese sauce over pasta and stir until well combined. Cover with bread crumbs. Bake at 350°F for 1 hour or until browned and bubbly.

Makes 8 servings

Home Cook's Hint

Semisoft cheeses, like Muenster and mozzarella are easier to shred if they are cold, so try placing them in the freezer for 10 to 15 minutes before shredding. To prevent cheese from becoming stringy when cooked, always use low heat and cook only until the cheese melts.

Ham 'n' Apple Breakfast Casserole Slices

Diane Halferty ◆ Corpus Christi, TX

1 package (15 ounces) refrigerated pie crusts (2 crusts)
20 pieces (about 1 pound) thinly sliced ham, cut into bite-size pieces
1 can (21 ounces) apple pie filling
1 cup (4 ounces) shredded sharp Cheddar cheese
¼ cup plus 1 teaspoon sugar, divided
½ teaspoon ground cinnamon

1. Preheat oven to 425°F.

2. Place one crust in 9-inch pie pan, allowing edges to hang over sides. Arrange half the ham slices on bottom crust. Spoon apple filling onto ham. Arrange remaining ham on top of apples; cover with cheese.

3. Mix ¼ cup sugar and cinnamon in small bowl; sprinkle evenly over cheese. Arrange second crust over filling and crimp edges together. Brush crust lightly with water and sprinkle with remaining 1 teaspoon sugar. Cut slits in top crust for steam to escape.

4. Bake 20 to 25 minutes or until crust is golden-brown. Cool 15 minutes. Slice into wedges.

Makes 6 servings

Diane says: This casserole can be assembled the night before, covered and refrigerated, then baked the next morning.

Italian Chicken My Way

Debbie Auterson ◆ Rio, CA

½ cup dry breadcrumbs
¼ cup grated Parmesan cheese
6 skinless boneless chicken breasts, cut in half lengthwise
4 tablespoons (½ stick) margarine
1 package (10 ounces) frozen chopped broccoli, thawed
1 teaspoon garlic powder
1 teaspoon Italian seasoning
1 jar (about 26 ounces) spaghetti sauce
2 cups (8 ounces) shredded mozzarella cheese

1. Preheat oven to 350°F. Combine bread crumbs and Parmesan cheese in shallow bowl. Place chicken breast halves one at a time in bread crumb mixture, pressing to coat both sides.

2. Heat margarine in large skillet over medium high heat. Cook chicken in batches until browned on both sides. Transfer chicken to a 13×9-inch casserole coated with nonstick cooking spray. Top with broccoli, sprinkle with garlic powder and Italian seasoning. Cover with spaghetti sauce; top with cheese.

3. Bake 25 minutes or until hot and bubbly and chicken is no longer pink in center.

Makes 12 servings

Home Cook's Hint

Thoroughly wash cutting surfaces, utensils and your hands with hot soapy water after coming in contact with uncooked chicken. This eliminates the risk of contaminating other foods with the salmonella bacteria that is often present in raw chicken. Salmonella is killed during cooking.

Cheesy Tuna Pie

Diane Nemitz ◆ Ludington, MI

2 cups cooked rice
2 cans (6 ounces each) tuna, drained and flaked
1 cup mayonnaise
1 cup (4 ounces) shredded Cheddar cheese
½ cup sour cream
½ cup thinly sliced celery
1 can (4 ounces) sliced black olives
2 tablespoons onion flakes
1 unbaked pie crust

1. Preheat oven to 350°F. Spray a 9-inch, deep-dish pie pan with nonstick cooking spray.

2. Combine all ingredients except pie crust in medium bowl; mix well. Spoon into prepared pie pan. Place pie crust over tuna mixture; press edges to pie pan to seal. Cut slits for steam to escape.

3. Bake 20 minutes or until crust is browned and filling is bubbly.

Makes 6 servings

Diane says: This is super easy! It uses ingredients I always have on hand, and I love the made-from-scratch flavor.

TEX-MEX FIESTA

Cha-Cha-Cha Casserole

Diane Halferty ◆ Corpus Christi, TX

1 can (about 7 ounces) whole green chilies, drained
1 pound ground turkey or chicken
1 cup chopped onion
1 tablespoon chili powder (or more to taste)
3 cloves garlic, minced
1 teaspoon ground cumin
1 teaspoon salt (optional)
1 can (10 ounces) diced tomatoes and green chilies, undrained
2 cups frozen corn, thawed, or 2 cups canned whole kernel corn, drained
1 can (16 ounces) refried beans
2 cups (8 ounces) shredded Mexican cheese blend
2 cups crushed tortilla chips
1 cup seeded diced fresh tomato
½ cup sliced green onions

1. Preheat oven to 375°F. Cut chilies in half lengthwise and arrange in single layer in 8-inch square baking dish coated with nonstick cooking spray.

2. Spray medium nonstick skillet with nonstick cooking spray. Cook and stir turkey, onion, chili powder, garlic, cumin and salt, if desired, over medium heat, until turkey is no longer pink. Add canned tomatoes and cook about 15 minutes until liquid evaporates.

3. Add meat mixture to casserole; top with corn, then beans. Sprinkle with cheese and crushed chips. Bake for 30 minutes; let stand 5 minutes before serving. Garnish with fresh tomatoes and green onions.

Makes 6 servings

Mexican Rice Olé

Kathy Schmalz ◆ *Westerville, OH*

1 teaspoon vegetable oil
1 cup uncooked long-grain rice
1 clove garlic, minced
1 teaspoon salt
1 can (about 14 ounces) chicken broth
1 can (10¾ ounces) condensed cream of onion soup, undiluted
¾ cup reduced-fat sour cream
1 can (4 ounces) chopped green chilies, undrained
⅓ cup prepared salsa
1 teaspoon ground cumin
1 cup (4 ounces) shredded Cheddar cheese
1 can (about 2 ounces) sliced black olives, drained

1. Preheat oven to 350°F. Coat 3-quart casserole with nonstick cooking spray.

2. Heat oil in large skillet over medium heat. Cook and stir rice, garlic and salt 2 or 3 minutes until rice is well coated. Add enough water to broth to equal 2 cups. Pour into skillet and simmer, stirring occasionally, about 15 minutes or until rice is tender.

3. Remove skillet from heat and add onion soup, sour cream, chilies, salsa and cumin; mix well. Spoon into prepared casserole; bake 20 minutes.

4. Top with cheese and olives. Bake additional 5 to 10 minutes until cheese melts and casserole is heated through.

Makes 4 servings

Kathy says: Cooked, chopped chicken may be added to make this casserole a one-dish meal.

Summer Fiesta Casserole

Barbara J. Johnson ◆ *Moses Lake, WA*

2 pounds ground beef
1 medium onion, chopped
1 package (about 1 ounce) taco seasoning mix
4 to 6 potatoes, peeled and cut into ½-inch cubes (about 4 cups)
1 to 2 tablespoons vegetable oil
4 cups sliced zucchini
1 can (14½ ounces) diced tomatoes with onion and garlic, undrained
1½ cups (6 ounces) shredded Mexican cheese blend

1. Preheat oven to 350°F. Spray 4-quart casserole with nonstick cooking spray.

2. Cook beef and onion in large skillet over medium heat until meat is no longer pink, stirring to separate meat; drain fat. Add taco seasoning and cook according to package directions. Transfer meat mixture to prepared casserole.

3. Add potatoes to same skillet; cook and stir over medium heat until potatoes are browned, adding oil as needed to prevent sticking. Add zucchini; cook and stir until beginning to soften. Transfer to casserole; top with tomatoes and cheese.

4. Bake 10 to 15 minutes or until cheese is melted and casserole is heated through.

Makes 4 to 6 servings

Barbara says: serve with tortilla chips, sour cream and salsa.

Esperanza's Enchiladas

Linda S. Killion Scott ◆ Santa Rosa, CA

　　1 cup vegetable oil
　12 corn tortillas, cut into 1-inch pieces
1½ to 2 pounds ground beef
　⅓ cup finely chopped yellow onion
　　1 can (10½ ounces) enchilada sauce
　　1 can (8 ounces) tomato sauce
　¼ cup water
　　1 envelope (about 1 ounce) taco or enchilada seasoning mix
　　2 cups (8 ounces) shredded mild Cheddar cheese
　　2 cups (8 ounces) shredded Monterey Jack cheese
　　1 can (6 ounces) black olives, drained and chopped
　　6 green onions, finely chopped
　　　Sour cream (optional)
　　　Guacamole (optional)

1. Preheat oven to 350°F.

2. Heat oil in medium skillet over medium-high heat. Add enough tortilla pieces to fill, but not crowd the skillet; fry until crisp. Remove with slotted spoon; set aside to drain on paper towels. Repeat with remaining tortilla pieces.

3. Cook and stir ground beef and onion in large skillet over medium-high heat stirring to break up meat until beef is browned; drain fat. Add enchilada sauce, tomato sauce, water and taco seasoning mix. Bring to a boil over high heat. Reduce heat to low and simmer 20 minutes.

4. Combine beef mixture with ⅔ of tortilla pieces in large bowl; transfer to 13×9-inch baking dish. Top with remaining ⅓ of tortilla pieces, cheeses, olives and green onions. Bake until cheeses are melted, about 5 to 10 minutes. Garnish with sour cream and guacamole, if desired.

Makes 6 to 8 servings

Home Cook's Hint

Save time and substitute a 1-pound bag of your favorite tortilla chips for the fried tortillas. For extra zing, substitute chorizo (a spicy Mexican sausage) for the ground beef.

Green Chile-Chicken Casserole

Lori Stokes ♦ *Odessa, TX*

4 cups shredded cooked chicken
1½ cups green enchilada sauce
1 can (10¾ ounces) condensed cream of chicken soup, undiluted
1 container (8 ounces) sour cream
1 can (4 ounces) diced green chilies
½ cup vegetable oil
12 (6-inch) corn tortillas
1½ cups (6 ounces) colby-jack cheese

1. Preheat oven to 325°F. Grease 13×9-inch casserole.

2. Combine chicken, enchilada sauce, soup, sour cream and chilies in large skillet over medium-high heat. Stir until warm.

3. In separate deep skillet heat oil. Fry tortillas just until soft, drain on paper towels. Place 4 tortillas on bottom of a prepared casserole. Layer with ⅓ chicken mixture and ½ cup cheese. Repeat layers twice.

4. Bake 15 to 20 minutes or until cheese is melted and casserole is heated through.

Makes 6 servings

Home Cook's Hint

Generally, a whole 3 to 4 pound chicken will yield about 4 cups cooked, boneless meat. If you wish to use boneless, skinless chicken breasts, you'll need about 1½ pounds of raw chicken to yield 4 cups of cooked meat.

Taco Casserole

Etta Delores Faultry ◆ *Alvin, TX*

2 pounds ground beef
1 teaspoon salt
1 teaspoon garlic powder
1 teaspoon cumin
1 teaspoon ground red pepper
1 teaspoon crushed red pepper flakes
1 teaspoon paprika
1 teaspoon chili powder
1 can (10 ounces) diced tomatoes and green chilies, undrained
1 bag (12 ounces) nacho cheese-flavored tortilla chips, crushed
½ cup chopped green onions
1 cup (4 ounces) shredded Mexican cheese blend
½ cup sour cream (optional)

1. Preheat oven to 375°F.

2. Combine beef, salt, garlic powder, cumin, ground red pepper, red pepper flakes, paprika and chili powder in large skillet. Cook and stir over medium high heat until meat is no longer pink. Drain fat.

3. Add tomatoes and chips; stir well. Transfer to 13×9-inch baking pan.

4. Bake 30 to 40 minutes or until bubbly. Sprinkle with onions and cheese. Top with sour cream, if desired.

Makes 4 to 6 servings

Picadillo Tamale Casserole

Julie DeMatteo ◆ *Clementon, NJ*

1½ pounds lean ground beef
1 cup chopped onion
2 cans (14½ ounces each) diced tomatoes with green chilies
½ cup chicken broth
½ teaspoon cinnamon
6 tablespoons slivered almonds
6 tablespoons raisins
2 rolls (1 pound each) prepared polenta, cut into ½-inch-thick slices
2 cups (8 ounces) shredded Mexican cheese blend

1. Preheat oven to 350°F.

2. Cook and stir beef and onion in large skillet over medium heat for 5 minutes or until meat is no longer pink; drain fat.

3. Add tomatoes, chicken broth and cinnamon; simmer 2 to 3 minutes. Stir in almonds and raisins.

4. Layer ½ of polenta slices, ½ of meat mixture and ½ of cheese in 13×9-inch casserole. Repeat layers.

5. Bake 25 to 30 minutes or until hot and bubbly.

Makes 8 servings

Cheesy Chicken Enchiladas

Julie DeMatteo · Clementon ◆ NJ

4 tablespoons (½ stick) butter or margarine
1 cup chopped onion
2 cloves garlic, minced
¼ cup all-purpose flour
1 cup chicken broth
4 ounces cream cheese, softened
2 cups (8 ounces) shredded Mexican cheese blend, divided
1 cup shredded cooked chicken
1 can (7 ounces) chopped green chilies, drained
½ cup diced pimientos
6 (8-inch) flour tortillas, warmed
¼ cup chopped fresh cilantro
¾ cup prepared salsa

1. Preheat oven to 350°F. Spray 13×9-inch baking dish with nonstick cooking spray.

2. Melt butter in medium saucepan over medium heat. Add onion and garlic; cook and stir until onion is tender. Add flour, cook and stir 1 minute. Gradually whisk in chicken broth; cook and stir 2 to 3 minutes or until slightly thickened. Add cream cheese; stir until melted. Stir in ½ cup shredded cheese, chicken, chilies and pimientos.

3. Spoon about ⅓ cup mixture onto each tortilla. Roll up and place in prepared baking dish seam-side down. Pour remaining mixture evenly on top and sprinkle with remaining 1½ cups shredded cheese.

4. Bake 20 minutes or until bubbly and lightly browned. Sprinkle with cilantro and serve with salsa.

Makes 6 servings

Taco Salad Casserole

Tammy Rose ◆ Princeton, WV

1 pound ground beef
1 cup chopped onion
1 can (15 ounces) chili with beans
1 can (14½ ounces) diced tomatoes, undrained
1 can (4 ounces) chopped green chilies, undrained
1 package (about 1 ounce) taco seasoning mix
1 bag (12 ounces) nacho chips, divided
2 cups (8 ounces) shredded Cheddar cheese
2 cups (8 ounces) shredded mozzarella cheese
3 to 4 cups shredded lettuce
1 jar (8 ounces) taco sauce
½ cup sour cream

1. Preheat oven to 350°F.

2. Cook and stir beef and onion in large skillet over medium heat until meat is no longer pink. Add chili with beans, tomatoes, green chilies and taco seasoning; cook and stir until heated through.

3. Crush nacho chips and place half in 2½-quart casserole. Pour meat mixture over chips and top with cheeses and remaining chips. Bake 30 to 40 minutes or until hot and bubbly.

4. Serve over bed of lettuce; top with taco sauce and sour cream.

Makes 6 to 8 servings

Zucornchile Rajas Bake

Elaine Sweet ◆ *Dallas, TX*

2 cups tomato sauce
2 tablespoons chili powder
2 tablespoons tomato paste
1 tablespoon cider vinegar
1 teaspoon ground cumin
½ teaspoon salt
½ teaspoon garlic powder
¼ teaspoon ground red pepper
6 corn tortillas
    Vegetable oil for frying
3 cups sliced zucchini
1½ cups (6 ounces) shredded Monterey Jack or manchego cheese, divided
1 cup corn kernels
1 can (4 ounces) diced green chiles, drained
½ to 1 cup sour cream
3 green onions, chopped

1. Preheat oven to 350°F. Oil 13×9-inch baking dish.

2. Combine tomato sauce, chili powder, tomato paste, vinegar, cumin, salt, garlic powder and red pepper. Bring to a boil over high heat; reduce heat to low and simmer 10 minutes, stirring occasionally.

3. Meanwhile, slice tortillas into ¼-inch strips. Heat enough oil to cover bottom of medium skillet by ½ inch. Fry tortilla strips in batches until crisp; drain on paper towels.

4. Steam zucchini for 5 minutes; drain. Transfer to large bowl. Add corn, chilies, ¾ cup cheese and tortilla strips. Toss lightly to combine; spoon into prepared baking dish. Spread tomato sauce mixture over zucchini mixture and top with remaining ¾ cup cheese. Bake 30 minutes or until heated through.

5. Spread sour cream over top and sprinkle with green onions. Serve immediately.

Makes 6 to 8 servings

VERY VEGGIE

 ## Vegetable Casserole

Adele Simoni ◆ Whiting, NJ

8 potatoes, peeled and cooked until tender
1 cup milk
¾ cup (1½ sticks) unsalted butter, divided
1 package (about 16 ounces) frozen spinach, cooked
   Salt and pepper
1 pound carrots, sliced, cooked until tender
1 pound string beans, cut into 1-inch pieces and cooked until tender
½ teaspoon paprika

1. Preheat oven to 375°F. Grease a 4-quart casserole or roasting pan.

2. Mash potatoes with milk and ½ cup butter until creamy. Set aside.

3. Spread spinach in casserole and dot with 1 tablespoon butter; season with salt and pepper.

4. Layer half of potatoes over spinach, followed by carrots and string beans. Dot with another 1 tablespoon butter; season with salt and pepper.

5. Layer remaining half of potatoes on top. Dot with remaining 2 tablespoons butter and sprinkle with paprika. Bake 1 hour or until heated through and lightly browned.

Makes 10 to 12 servings

Crunchy Top & Flaky Bottom Broccoli Casserole

Gloria Herdman ◆ Pomeroy, OH

2 cans (8 ounces each) refrigerated crescent roll dough
1 package (16 ounces) frozen chopped broccoli
2 cups (8 ounces) shredded mozzarella cheese, divided
1½ cups French fried onions, coarsely crushed and divided
1 can (10¾ ounces) condensed cream of mushroom soup, undiluted
2 cans (5 ounces each) lean ham, drained and flaked
½ cup mayonnaise
2 eggs, beaten
2 tablespoons Dijon mustard
1 tablespoon prepared horseradish
1 jar (2 ounces) chopped pimientos, drained
1 teaspoon finely chopped parsley

1. Preheat oven to 375°F. Butter bottom of 13×9-inch baking dish. Unroll cans of dough; do not separate. Press dough onto bottom of prepared baking dish, sealing all seams. Bake 7 minutes; remove from oven and set aside.

2. Combine broccoli, 1 cup cheese, ½ cup onions, soup, ham, mayonnaise, eggs, mustard and horseradish. Spread evenly over crust. Top with remaining 1 cup onions, 1 cup cheese, pimientos and parsley.

3. Bake for 20 to 25 minutes or until set. Cool 10 minutes before serving.

Makes 8 servings

Southwest Spaghetti Squash

Lynda McCormick ◆ Burkburnett, TX

1 spaghetti squash (about 2 pounds)
1 can (about 15 ounces) Mexican-style diced tomatoes, undrained
1 can (about 15 ounces) black beans, rinsed and drained
¾ cup (3 ounces) shredded Monterey Jack cheese, divided
¼ cup finely chopped cilantro
1 teaspoon cumin
¼ teaspoon garlic salt
¼ teaspoon freshly ground black pepper

1. Preheat oven to 350°F. Cut squash in half lengthwise. Remove and discard seeds. Place squash, cut side down, on greased baking pan. Bake 45 minutes to 1 hour or until just tender. Using fork, remove spaghetti-like strands from hot squash and place strands in large bowl. (Use oven mitts to protect hands.)

2. Add tomatoes, beans, ½ cup cheese, cilantro, cumin, garlic salt and pepper to squash and stir well.

2. Spoon into a 1½-quart casserole sprayed with nonstick cooking spray. Sprinkle with remaining ¼ cup cheese.

3. Bake, uncovered 30 to 35 minutes or until heated through. Serve immediately.

Makes 4 servings

Lynda says: This is a very simple dish you can throw together in a few minutes, then bake. Great for those nights you want to go meatless! Also a "kid-friendly" meal.

Baked Risotto with Asparagus, Spinach & Parmesan

June Holmes ◆ *Alpharetta, GA*

1 cup finely chopped onion
1 tablespoon olive oil
1 cup arborio (risotto) rice
8 cups (8 to 10 ounces) spinach leaves, torn into pieces
2 cups chicken broth
¼ teaspoon salt
¼ teaspoon ground nutmeg
½ cup Parmesan cheese, divided
1½ cups diagonally sliced asparagus

1. Preheat oven to 400°F. Spray 13×9-inch baking dish with nonstick cooking spray.

2. In large skillet heat olive oil over medium high heat; cook and stir onion 4 minutes or until tender. Add rice and stir well.

3. Stir in spinach, a handful at a time, adding more as it wilts. Add broth, salt and nutmeg. Reduce heat and simmer 7 minutes. Stir in ¼ cup cheese.

5. Transfer to prepared baking dish. Cover tightly and bake 15 minutes.

6. Remove from oven and stir in asparagus; sprinkle with remaining ¼ cup cheese. Cover and bake 15 minutes more or until liquid is absorbed.

Makes 6 servings

Home Cook's Hint

Classic Italian risotto is easy to make and delicious, but it does require a special short-grain, high-starch rice. Arborio is the most readily available. Never rinse arborio rice before cooking since you don't want to wash off the starchy coating which makes the finished dish creamy.

Polynesian Baked Beans

Lynda McCormick ◆ Burkburnett, TX

2 tablespoons olive oil
3 tablespoons chopped onion
2 cans (16 ounces each) baked beans
1 can (about 11 ounces) mandarin oranges, drained
1 can (about 8 ounces) pineapple chunks in juice, drained
½ cup chopped green bell pepper
1 can (about 4 ounces) deviled ham
¼ cup ketchup
2 tablespoons packed brown sugar
½ teaspoon salt (optional)
   Dash hot pepper sauce

1. Preheat oven to 375°F. Heat oil in small skillet over medium heat. Add onion; cook and stir until transparent.

2. Combine onion and remaining ingredients in 2-quart casserole. Bake, uncovered, 30 to 35 minutes or until bubbly.

Makes 6 to 8 servings

Lynda says: This is a great recipe to double and can also be made in a slow cooker.

Home Cook's Hint

Don't throw away the juice drained from canned pineapple. Add it to your morning orange juice for a nice change, or use it in a marinade or salad dressing. Pineapple juice is an excellent ingredient for many marinades since it contains an enzyme that is a natural tenderizer.

Party Potatoes

Tami Crosby ◆ Glendale, AZ

1 bag (32 ounces) Southern-style hash browns
2 cans (10¾ ounces each) condensed cream of potato soup, undiluted
2 cups (16 ounces) sour cream
2 cups (8 ounces) shredded Cheddar cheese
¾ red onion, finely chopped
¼ cup (½ stick) butter, sliced
   Parmesan cheese (optional)

1. Preheat oven to 350°F. Grease 13×9-inch baking dish.

2. Combine hash browns, soup, sour cream and Cheddar cheese and onion. Spoon evenly in baking dish and pat down.

3. Arrange butter slices on top and sprinkle with Parmesan cheese, if desired.

4. Cover with foil; bake 60 minutes. Remove foil and bake an additional 10 minutes or until browned.

Makes 10 servings

Broccoli Casserole

Dorothy Cummings ◆ Gore, OK

1 package (about 6 ounces) stuffing mix
1 can (10¾ ounces) condensed cream of mushroom soup, undiluted
1 package (10 ounces) frozen chopped broccoli, thawed
½ small onion, chopped
½ cup (2 ounces) shredded mozzarella cheese

1. Preheat oven to 350°F. Grease 2-quart casserole.

2. Prepare stuffing mix according to package directions. Add soup, broccoli, and onion; mix well. Pour into prepared dish. Cover with cheese.

3. Bake 30 minutes or until heated through and cheese melts.

Makes 4 servings

Fruited Corn Pudding

Carole Resnick ◆ *Cleveland, OH*

5 cups frozen corn, thawed and divided
5 eggs
½ cup milk
1½ cups heavy cream
⅓ cup unsalted butter, melted and cooled
1 teaspoon vanilla
½ teaspoon salt
¼ teaspoon ground nutmeg
3 tablespoons dried cranberries or raisins
3 tablespoons finely chopped dates
3 tablespoons finely chopped dried apricots
2 tablespoons finely chopped dried pears, or other dried fruit

1. Preheat oven to 350°F. Butter a 13×9-inch baking dish; set aside.

2. In food processor, combine 3½ cups corn, eggs, and milk; process until mixture is almost smooth.

3. Transfer corn mixture to large bowl. Add cream, butter, vanilla, salt and nutmeg; stir until well combined. Add remaining 1½ cups corn, cranberries, dates, apricots and pears. Stir well. Pour mixture into baking dish.

4. Bake until custard is set and top begins to brown, about 50 to 60 minutes. Remove from oven and allow to sit for 10 to 15 minutes before serving.

Makes 8 to 10 servings

Home Cook's Hint

To make chopping dried fruit easier, spray the knife or food processor blade with nonstick cooking spray before beginning. Placing the fruit in the freezer an hour ahead of time aids chopping, too. Some dried fruits, like apricots, are easier to snip with a kitchen shears than to chop with a knife.

Spinach Casserole

Charlotte G Williams ◆ *St. Clair, PA*

3 tablespoons butter
1 tablespoon flour
1 cup milk
2 eggs, separated
1 tablespoon chopped fresh parsley
  Salt and pepper
1 cup (4 ounces) shredded Cheddar cheese
2 packages (14 ounces each) frozen chopped spinach, thawed and
    squeezed dry

1. Preheat oven to 350°F. Butter 2½ quart casserole.

2. Melt butter in medium saucepan over medium heat. Stir in flour and cook and stir 2 minutes. Gradually whisk in milk. Continue cooking until mixture thickens slightly. Gradually add egg yolks. Season with parsley, salt and pepper. Add cheese, stirring constantly until cheese melts. Transfer to medium bowl.

3. Add spinach to cheese sauce and stir until well combined; keep warm. Meanwhile, beat egg whites to stiff peaks in clean, dry bowl. Gently fold egg whites into spinach-cheese mixture.

4. Spoon into prepared casserole and bake 40 minutes or until center is set and looks dry. *Do not overbake.*

Makes 6 servings

Spanish Rice & Squash

Charlotte Sue Taylor ◆ Midway, WV

2 small yellow summer squash, cut into ¼-inch slices
1 small zucchini, cut into ¼-inch slices
1 package (about 12 ounces) Spanish rice mix
2 cups water
1 can (about 14 ounces) diced tomatoes, undrained
1 can (about 4 ounces) sliced mushrooms
3 tablespoons butter, melted
1 pound smoked sausage, cut into 4-inch pieces
1 can (about 3 ounces) French fried onions
1 cup shredded mozzarella cheese

1. Preheat oven to 350°F. Coat 3-quart casserole with nonstick cooking spray. Place sliced squash and zucchini in prepared casserole.

2. Combine rice mix, water, tomatoes, mushrooms and butter in medium bowl; stir well. Pour over squash; top with sausage.

3. Cover and bake 20 minutes. Remove from oven; uncover and place onions around edge of casserole. Sprinkle cheese in center. Bake, uncovered, 5 to 10 minutes or until cheese melts.

Makes 4 to 6 servings

Carrie's Sweet Potato Casserole

Carrie Anderson ◆ *Hyattsville, MD*

Topping (recipe follows)
6 cups (about 3 pounds) cooked and peeled sweet potatoes
½ cup (1 stick) butter, softened
1 teaspoon vanilla
½ cup sugar
2 eggs, beaten
½ cup evaporated milk
1 cup pecans, chopped

1. Prepare topping; set aside. Preheat oven to 350°F. Grease 13×9-inch baking dish.

2. Mash sweet potatoes with butter in large bowl. Beat with electric mixer until light and fluffy.

3. One at a time, add vanilla, sugar, eggs and evaporated milk, beating after each addition. Pour into prepared baking dish. Spoon on topping and sprinkle with pecans.

4. Bake 25 minutes or until heated through. Serve hot.

Makes 12 to 14 servings

Topping: Combine 1 cup packed brown sugar, ½ cup all-purpose flour and ⅓ cup melted butter in medium bowl.

Home Cook's Hint

This casserole works well and looks pretty in individual-size serving dishes. To prepare single-servings, grease 8 (6-ounce) oven-proof ramekins and fill them almost to the top with the sweet potato mixture. Top as in step 3 of the recipe. Bake at 350°F about 20 minutes or until heated through.

Summer Squash Casserole

Darleen Presnell ◆ *Deep Gap, NC*

2 cups sliced yellow summer squash
1 medium carrot, thinly sliced
½ cup chopped onion
½ cup diced red or green bell pepper
½ teaspoon salt
⅛ teaspoon pepper
1 container (8 ounces) sour cream
1 can (10¾ ounces) condensed cream of chicken or mushroom soup,
   undiluted
1 cup (4 ounces) shredded Italian cheese blend
1 cup (4 ounces) shredded Cheddar cheese
1 package (6 ounces) stuffing mix

1. Preheat oven to 350°F. Combine squash, carrot, onion, bell pepper, salt and pepper in a medium saucepan; cover with water. Bring to a boil and cook 5 minutes or until tender. Drain.

2. Combine sour cream and soup in 13×9-inch casserole; mix well. Stir in vegeatable mixture and spread evenly. Sprinkle cheeses on top.

3. Top with dry stuffing mix. Bake 30 minutes or until heated through.

Makes 6 servings

Wild Rice Casserole

Philip A. Pinchotti ◆ *Freedom, PA*

1 cup wild rice, soaked overnight
1 large onion, chopped
1 cup shredded Cheddar cheese
1 cup chopped mushrooms
1 cup chopped black olives
1 cup drained chopped canned tomatoes
1 cup tomato juice
⅓ cup vegetable oil
   Salt and pepper

1. Preheat oven to 350°F.

2. Drain rice. Combine rice and remaining ingredients, except salt and pepper, in large bowl.

3. Season with salt and pepper. Transfer to casserole. Cover and bake 1½ hours, or until rice is tender.

Makes 6 servings

Philip says: *This tastes even better reheated the next day.*

PASTA PERFECT

Italian Tomato Bake

Terry Lunday ◆ Flagstaff, AZ

1 pound sweet Italian sausage, cut into ½-inch slices
2 tablespoons margarine or butter
1 cup chopped onion
4 cups cooked egg noodles
2 cups prepared pasta sauce
2 cups frozen broccoli florets
½ cup diced tomatoes
2 cloves garlic, minced
3 Roma tomatoes, sliced
1 cup (8 ounces) low-fat ricotta cheese
⅓ cup grated Parmesan cheese
1 teaspoon dried oregano

1. Preheat oven to 350°F. Cook sausage in skillet over medium heat about 10 minutes or until barely pink in center. Remove, drain on paper towels and reserve. Drain fat from skillet.

2. Add margarine and onion to skillet; cook and stir until onion is tender. Meanwhile, steam broccoli 5 minutes until crisp-tender; drain. Combine onion, noodles, pasta sauce, broccoli, diced tomatoes and garlic in large bowl; mix well.

3. Transfer to 13×9-inch baking dish. Top with cooked sausage and arrange tomato slices over top. Place 1 heaping tablespoon ricotta cheese on each tomato slice. Sprinkle casserole with Parmesan cheese and oregano. Bake 35 minutes or until hot and bubbly.

Makes 6 servings

Bow Tie Zucchini

Karen Tellier ◆ *Cumberland, RI*

¼ cup vegetable oil
1 cup chopped onion
2 cloves garlic, minced
5 small zucchini, cut into thin strips
⅔ cup heavy cream
1 package (16 ounces) bow tie pasta, cooked and drained
3 tablespoons grated Parmesan cheese
Salt and pepper

1. Preheat oven to 350°F.

2. Heat oil in large skillet over medium-high heat. Add onion and garlic; cook and stir until onion is tender. Add zucchini; cook and stir until tender.

2. Add cream; cook and stir until thickened. Add pasta and cheese to skillet. Season with salt and pepper to taste. Transfer mixture to 2-quart casserole. Cover and bake 15 minutes or until heated through.

Makes 8 servings

Home Cook's Hint

When pasta will be added to a casserole or cooked longer with other ingredients, it's very important not to overcook it in the first place. Don't necessarily trust the cooking times printed on the package. They sometimes produce limp, soggy noodles. The best way to test pasta is to remove a piece and taste it. It should still be a bit firm, but not chalky or hard in the middle.

Bow Tie Zucchini

Seafood Pasta

Rita Berger ◆ *Wauconda, IL*

½ cup olive oil
1 pound asparagus, cut into 1-inch pieces
1 cup chopped green onions
5 teaspoons chopped garlic
1 package (about 16 ounces) linguine, cooked and drained
1 pound medium shrimp, cooked, shelled and deveined
1 package (about 8 ounces) imitation crabmeat
1 package (about 8 ounces) imitation lobster
1 can (about 6 ounces) sliced black olives, drained

1. Preheat oven to 350°F. Spray 4-quart casserole with nonstick cooking spray. Heat oil in large skillet over medium heat. Cook and stir asparagus, green onions and garlic until tender.

2. Combine asparagus mixture, cooked linguine, seafood and olives in prepared casserole. Bake 30 minutes or until heated through.

Makes 6 servings

Crunchy Tuna Casserole

Carol Galbreath ◆ *Avon, IN*

1 can (10¾ ounces) condensed cream of chicken soup, undiluted
6 ounces medium noodles or macaroni, cooked and drained
1 can (6 ounces) tuna, drained and flaked
1 cup (4 ounces) shredded sharp Cheddar cheese
½ cup sliced celery
½ cup milk
¼ cup mayonnaise
1 can (4 ounces) sliced water chestnuts, drained
1 jar (2 ounces) chopped pimientos, drained
½ teaspoon salt
   Dash pepper
   Pinch celery seeds

1. Preheat oven to 425°F. Spray 2-quart casserole with nonstick cooking spray.

2. Combine all ingredients in prepared casserole. Bake 25 minutes or until hot and bubbly.

Makes 6 servings

Mom's Baked Mostaccioli

Lynda McCormick ◆ Burkburnett, TX

　　1 container (16 ounces) part-skim ricotta cheese
　½ cup egg substitute
　¼ cup grated Parmesan cheese
　　Garlic powder
　　Pepper
　　Italian seasoning
　　1 package (16 ounces) mostaccioli, cooked and drained
　　1 jar (26 ounces) prepared spaghetti sauce
　1½ cups (6 ounces) shredded mozzarella cheese

1. Preheat oven to 350°F. Spray 13×9-inch casserole with nonstick cooking spray.

2. Combine ricotta cheese, egg substitute and Parmesan cheese in medium bowl. Season with garlic powder, pepper and Italian seasoning; mix well.

3. Place half of pasta in prepared casserole. Spread ricotta mixture evenly over pasta. Spoon remaining pasta over ricotta mixture. Top with spaghetti sauce and mozzarella cheese.

4. Bake 30 minutes or until hot and bubbly.

Makes 8 servings

Manicotti

Billie Olofson ◆ Des Moines, IA

1 container (16 ounces) ricotta cheese
2 cups (8 ounces) shredded mozzarella cheese
½ cup cottage cheese
2 tablespoons grated Parmesan cheese
2 eggs, beaten
½ teaspoon minced garlic
   Salt and pepper
1 package (16 ounces) manicotti shells, uncooked
1 pound ground beef
1 jar (28 ounces) spaghetti sauce
2 cups water

1. Combine ricotta cheese, mozzarella cheese, cottage cheese, Parmesan cheese, eggs and garlic in large bowl; mix well. Season with salt and pepper.

2. Stuff mixture into uncooked manicotti shells using rubber spatula. Place filled shells in 13×9-inch baking dish. Preheat oven to 375°F.

3. Cook ground beef in large skillet over medium-high heat until no longer pink, stirring to separate. Drain off excess fat. Stir in spaghetti sauce and water (mixture will be thin). Pour sauce over filled manicotti shells.

4. Cover with foil; bake 1 hour or until sauce has thickened and shells are tender.

Makes 6 servings

Home Cook's Hint

It's much easier to stuff uncooked pasta shells than boiled ones. As long as the pasta is covered with enough liquid, it will cook right in the sauce in the oven and save the step of boiling it first. Many lasagna recipes can also be prepared this way with uncooked lasagna noodles.

Ravioli Casserole

Carrie Mae Anderson ◆ *Hyattsville, MD*

1 pound lean ground beef
2 tablespoons dried onion flakes
2 teaspoons soy sauce
¼ teaspoon dried minced garlic
2 packages (10 ounces each) frozen chopped spinach, thawed
1 jar (16 ounces) prepared spaghetti sauce
1 can (8 ounces) tomato sauce
1 can (6 ounces) tomato paste
1 tablespoon barbecue sauce
1 teaspoon Italian salad dressing
½ teaspoon dried oregano
¼ teaspoon pepper
1 package (7 ounces) macaroni, cooked
2 cups (8 ounces) shredded sharp Cheddar cheese
½ cup bread crumbs
2 eggs, beaten
¼ cup vegetable oil

1. Preheat oven to 350°F. Spray 13×9-inch casserole with nonstick cooking spray. Cook ground beef, onion, soy sauce and garlic in large skillet over medium heat 5 minutes or until no longer pink. Stir in spinach, spaghetti sauce, tomato sauce, tomato paste, barbecue sauce, salad dressing, oregano and pepper. Reduce heat to low; simmer 10 minutes.

2. Combine cooked macaroni, cheese, bread crumbs, eggs and oil in large bowl; mix well. Spread evenly in bottom of prepared casserole; top with beef mixture.

3. Bake 30 minutes or until hot and bubbly.

Makes 8 to 10 servings

Pasta & White Bean Casserole

Julie DeMatteo ◆ *Clementon, NJ*

½ cup chopped onion

2 cloves garlic, minced

1 tablespoon olive oil

2 cans (about 15 ounces each) cannellini beans, drained and rinsed

3 cups cooked small shell pasta

1 can (8 ounces) tomato sauce

1½ teaspoons dried Italian seasoning

½ teaspoon salt

½ teaspoon pepper

1 cup (4 ounces) shredded Italian cheese blend

2 tablespoons finely chopped parsley

1. Preheat oven to 350°F. Spray 2-quart casserole with nonstick cooking spray. Cook onion and garlic in oil in large skillet over medium-high heat 3 to 4 minutes or until onion is tender.

2. Add beans, pasta, tomato sauce, Italian seasoning, salt and pepper; mix well. Transfer to prepared casserole; sprinkle with cheese and parsley. Bake 20 minutes or until cheese is melted.

Makes 6 servings

Home Cook's Hint

To cook pasta perfectly you need plenty of rapidly boiling salted water—4 to 6 quarts for 1 pound of pasta. Cook pasta at a full boil and stir occasionally for even cooking and to prevent sticking. Check doneness at minimum suggested time by removing a piece and tasting.

Tuscan Baked Rigatoni

Julie DeMatteo ◆ *Clementon, NJ*

1 pound Italian sausage, casings removed
1 pound rigatoni pasta, cooked, drained and kept warm
2 cups (8 ounces) shredded fontina cheese
2 tablespoons olive oil
2 fennel bulbs, thinly sliced
4 cloves garlic, minced
1 can (28 ounce) crushed tomatoes
1 cup heavy cream
1 teaspoon salt
1 teaspoon pepper
8 cups coarsely chopped spinach
1 can (15 ounces) cannellini beans, rinsed and drained
2 tablespoons pine nuts
½ cup grated Parmesan cheese

1. Preheat oven to 350°F. Spray 4-quart casserole with nonstick cooking spray. Crumble sausage in large skillet over medium-high heat. Cook and stir until no longer pink; drain. Transfer sausage to large bowl. Add cooked pasta and Fontina cheese; mix well.

2. Combine oil, fennel and garlic in same skillet. Cook and stir over medium heat 3 minutes or until fennel is tender. Add tomatoes, cream, salt and pepper; cook and stir until slightly thickened. Stir in spinach, beans and pine nuts; cook until heated through.

3. Pour sauce over pasta and sausage; toss to coat. Transfer to prepared casserole; sprinkle evenly with Parmesan cheese. Bake 30 minutes or hot and bubbly.

Makes 6 to 8 servings

ONE-DISH DINNERS

Saffron Chicken & Vegetables

Brenda Melancon ◆ Bay St. Louis, MS

2 tablespoons vegetable oil
6 bone-in chicken thighs, skinned
1 bag (16 ounces) frozen mixed vegetables, such as broccoli, red peppers, mushrooms and onions, thawed
1 can (14½ ounces) roasted garlic flavor chicken broth
1 can (10¾ ounces) condensed cream of chicken soup, undiluted
1 can condensed cream of mushroom soup, undiluted
1 package (8 ounces) saffron yellow rice mix with seasonings
½ cup water
½ teaspoon salt
1 teaspoon paprika (optional)

1. Preheat oven to 350°F. Spray 3-quart casserole with nonstick cooking spray; set aside.

2. Heat oil in large skillet over medium heat. Add chicken and cook 10 minutes or until no longer pink in center; drain fat.

3. Meanwhile, combine vegetables, chicken broth, soups, rice mix with seasonings, water and salt in large bowl. Place mixture in prepared casserole. Top with chicken. Sprinkle with paprika, if desired. Cover and bake 1½ hours.

Makes 6 servings

Thyme for Chicken Stew with Polenta Dumplings

Diane Halferty ◆ *Corpus Christi, TX*

2 pounds boneless skinless chicken thighs
4 tablespoons olive oil, divided
2 medium eggplants, chopped
6 small onions
4 tomatoes, seeded and diced
½ cup chicken broth
⅓ cup pitted black olives, sliced
1 tablespoon chopped fresh thyme *or* 1 teaspoon dried thyme leaves
1 tablespoon red wine vinegar
Dumplings (recipe follows)

1. Preheat oven to 350°F. Rinse chicken and pat dry with paper towels. Heat 1 tablespoon oil over medium-high heat in 4-quart Dutch oven. Cook chicken in batches 4 to 5 minutes or until browned on all sides. Remove and set aside.

2. Heat remaining 3 tablespoons oil in same Dutch oven; add eggplant, onions and tomatoes. Reduce heat to medium. Cook, stirring occasionally, 5 minutes. Return chicken to Dutch oven. Add chicken broth, olives, thyme and vinegar; stir to combine. Bring to a boil. Transfer to oven; bake uncovered 1 hour. Meanwhile, prepare Dumplings.

3. Remove stew from oven; top with rounded tablespoonfuls dumpling mixture. Bake uncovered about 20 minutes or until dumplings are cooked through.

Makes 6 servings

Dumplings: Bring 3½ cups chicken broth to a boil in medium saucepan over medium-high heat. Gradually whisk in 1 cup polenta or yellow cornmeal. Reduce heat to low; simmer, stirring, about 15 minutes until thickened. Remove from heat; stir in 1 egg, 2 tablespoons butter, ½ cup grated Parmesan cheese and ¼ cup diced parsley.

Tuna Tomato Casserole

Cortney Morford ◆ Tuckahoe, NJ

2 cans (6 ounces each) chunk light tuna, drained
1 cup mayonnaise
1 small onion, finely chopped
¼ teaspoon salt
¼ teaspoon black pepper
1 bag (12 ounces) wide egg noodles
8 to 10 plum tomatoes, sliced ¼ inch thick
1 cup (4 ounces) shredded Cheddar or mozzarella cheese

1. Preheat oven to 375°F.

1. Combine tuna, mayonnaise, onion, salt and pepper in medium bowl. Mix well and set aside.

2. Prepare noodles according to package directions, cooking just until tender. Drain noodles and return to pot.

3. Add tuna mixture to noodles; stir until well combined.

4. Layer half noodle mixture, half tomatoes and half cheese in 13×9-inch baking dish. Press down slightly. Repeat layers with remaining ingredients.

5. Bake 20 minutes or until cheese is melted and browned.

Makes 6 servings

Sunday Dinner Casserole

Ronda Tucker ◆ *Ten Mile, TN*

½ cup cooking sherry
2 tablespoons sugar
2 tablespoons balsamic vinegar
1 teaspoon dried thyme leaves
½ teaspoon black pepper
2 cups sweet onion rings
2 cups egg noodles, cooked
2 pounds boneless skinless chicken breasts
3 cups chicken broth
1 can (14½ ounces) diced tomatoes, drained
2 cloves garlic minced
½ teaspoon crushed red pepper
2 teaspoons lemon zest
¼ cup chopped fresh basil

1. Preheat oven to 400°F.

2. Combine sherry, sugar, vinegar, thyme and black pepper in large skillet. Add onions; stir to coat. Cook, stirring occassionally over medium heat until onions begin to brown.

3. Meanwhile, place noodles in 13×9-inch baking pan. Top with chicken breasts. Combine broth, tomatoes, garlic and red pepper with onions in skillet. Pour over chicken-noodle mixture in baking pan.

4. Bake, uncovered 20 minutes; turn chicken breasts. Bake additional 20 to 25 minutes or until chicken is no longer pink in center and juices run clear. Sprinkle with lemon zest and basil.

Makes 4 to 6 servings.

Crab, Shrimp & Zucchini Baked Delight

Louise A Donavant ◆ Bellevue, WA

2 medium zucchini
1 cup flaked fresh crab
1 cup small fresh bay shrimp
1 cup sour cream
⅓ cup sliced green pimento-stuffed olives
1 tablespoon finely chopped onion
1 tablespoon finely chopped green bell pepper
1 tablespoon fresh lemon juice
2 cups (8 ounces) shredded Cheddar cheese
Paprika and parsley sprigs, for garnish (optional)

1. Preheat oven to 300°F. Butter 8×10-inch baking dish

2. Place whole zucchini in saucepan of boiling water. Boil 3 to 5 minutes or just until tender. Cool slightly. Cut zucchini in half lengthwise. Scoop out seeds and some of flesh; discard seeds and flesh. Place in prepared baking dish, cut-side up.

3. Combine crab, shrimp, sour cream, olives, onion, bell pepper and lemon juice in large bowl; mix well. Place ¼ of crab mixture in each zucchini half. Top each half with ½ cup cheese.

4. Bake 1 hour or until lightly browned. Garnish with paprika and parsley sprigs, if desired.

Makes 4 servings

Easy Moroccan Casserole

April Parmelee ◆ Anaheim, CA

　　2 tablespoons vegetable oil
　　1 pound pork stew meat, cut into 1-inch cubes
　½ cup chopped onion
　　3 tablespoons all-purpose flour
　　1 can (16 ounces) diced tomatoes, undrained
　¼ cup water
　　1 teaspoon ground ginger
　　1 teaspoon ground cumin
　　1 teaspoon ground cinnamon
　½ teaspoon sugar
　½ teaspoon salt
　½ teaspoon black pepper
　　2 medium red potatoes, unpeeled, cut into ½-inch pieces
　　1 large sweet potato, unpeeled, cut into ½-inch pieces
　　1 cup frozen lima beans, thawed and drained
　　1 cup frozen cut green beans, thawed and drained
　¾ cup sliced carrots
　　　Pita bread

1. Preheat oven to 325°F.

2. Heat oil in large skillet over medium-high heat. Add pork and onion; cook, stirring occasionally, until pork is browned on all sides.

3. Sprinkle flour over meat mixture in skillet. Stir until flour has absorbed pan juices. Cook 2 minutes more.

4. Stir in tomatoes with juice, water, ginger, cumin, cinnamon, sugar, salt and pepper. Transfer mixture to 2-quart casserole. Bake 30 minutes.

5. Stir in potatoes, sweet potato, lima beans, green beans and carrots. Cover and bake 1 hour or until potatoes are tender. Serve with pita bread.

Makes 6 servings

Seafood Newburg Casserole

Julie De Matteo ◆ Clementon, NJ

1 can (10¾ ounces) condensed cream of shrimp soup, undiluted
½ cup half-and-half
1 tablespoon dry sherry
¼ teaspoon ground red pepper
3 cups cooked rice
2 cans (6 ounces each) lump crabmeat, drained
¼ pound medium shrimp, peeled and deveined
¼ pound bay scallops
1 jar (4 ounces) pimientos, drained and chopped
¼ cup finely chopped parsley

1. Preheat oven to 350°F. Spray 2½-quart casserole with nonstick cooking spray.

2. Whisk together soup, half-and-half, sherry and red pepper in large bowl until combined. Add rice, crab, shrimp, scallops and pimientos; toss well.

3. Transfer to prepared casserole; sprinkle with parsley. Cover and bake about 25 minutes or until shrimp and scallops are opaque.

Makes 6 servings

Home Cook's Hint

When buying scallops look for those with a sweet smell and a cream or pinkish color. If scallops are pure white, chances are they've been treated with a chemical to make them look fresh longer. Bay scallops are smaller and more expensive than sea scallops. Overcooking any scallop can make it rubbery and tough.

Beef in Wine Sauce

Tamara Frazier ◆ Escondido, CA

4 pounds boneless beef chuck, cut into 1½- to 2-inch cubes
2 tablespoons garlic powder
2 cans (10¾ ounces each) condensed golden mushroom soup, undiluted
1 envelope (about 1 ounce) onion soup mix
¾ cup dry sherry
1 can (8 ounces) sliced mushrooms, drained
1 bag (20 ounces) frozen sliced carrots

1. Preheat oven to 325°F. Spray heavy 4-quart casserole or Dutch oven with nonstick cooking spray.

2. Sprinkle beef with garlic powder. Place in casserole.

3. Combine mushroom soup, onion soup mix, sherry and mushrooms in medium bowl. Pour over meat; mix well.

4. Cover casserole and bake 3 hours or until meat is very tender. Add carrots during last 15 minutes of baking.

Makes 6 to 8 servings

Home Cook's Hint

Cooking a tough cut of meat, like beef chuck, for a long time at low heat with a little liquid is often called braising. It's a good way to get maximum flavor and tenderness from less expensive cuts. For best results, braise in a sturdy, heavy casserole that retains heat and spreads it evenly through the contents.

City Chicken BBQ Casserole

Jan Blue ◆ Cuyahoga Falls, OH

2 tablespoons vegetable oil
6 to 8 boneless pork* chops (about 2 pounds), cut into bite-size pieces
¼ cup chopped onions
2 cloves garlic, chopped
2 cups water
2 cups uncooked instant white rice
2 cups shredded mozzarella cheese

Sauce:

1 bottle (12 ounces) chili sauce
1 cup ketchup
½ cup packed brown sugar
2 tablespoons honey
1 tablespoon Worcestershire sauce
1 tablespoon hot pepper jelly
1 teaspoon ground ginger
1 teaspoon liquid smoke (optional)
½ teaspoon curry powder
¼ teaspoon black pepper

Note: "City chicken" is a traditional dish in Ohio and Pennsylvania. The name indicates that chicken was once a more expensive food than pork, so the cheaper cuts were prepared to taste like chicken.

1. Preheat oven to 350°F.

2. Heat oil in large skillet over medium-high heat until hot. Add pork; cook and stir 10 to 15 minutes until browned and no longer pink in center. Add onions and garlic; cook until onions are tender. Drain fat.

3. Meanwhile, bring water to a boil in small saucepan. Stir in rice; cover. Remove from heat; let stand 5 minutes or until water is absorbed.

4. Combine sauce ingredients in separate saucepan; bring to a boil. Reduce heat to low; cover and simmer 10 minutes, stirring occasionally.

5. Combine pork mixture, rice and sauce in 2½-quart casserole; mix well. Bake 15 to 20 minutes. Top with mozzarella cheese and bake 5 minutes more or until heated through and cheese melts.

Makes 6 to 8 servings

City Chicken BBQ Casserole

Escalloped Chicken

Billie Olofson ◆ *Des Moines, IA*

10 slices white bread, cubed
1½ cups cracker or dry bread crumbs, divided
4 cups cubed cooked chicken
1 cup chopped onion
1 cup chopped celery
3 cups chicken broth
1 can (8 ounces) sliced mushrooms, drained
1 jar (about 4 ounces) diced pimientos, drained
3 eggs, lightly beaten
1 tablespoon margarine
Salt and pepper

1. Preheat oven to 350°F.

2. Combine bread cubes and 1 cup cracker crumbs in large mixing bowl. Add chicken, onion, celery, broth, mushrooms, pimientos and eggs; mix well. Spoon into 2½-quart casserole.

3. Melt margarine in small saucepan. Add remaining ½ cup cracker crumbs and brown, stirring occasionally. Sprinkle crumbs over casserole.

4. Bake 1 hour, until hot and bubbly.

Makes 6 servings

Home Cook's Hint

Bread and cracker crumbs are often used as casserole toppings. While they can be purchased, they are easy to make and a good use for stale bread. Trim the edges of the slices if you like. Place in a food processor or blender and process until fine. One average slice of bread makes about ½ cup of crumbs.

Ham Jambalaya

Margaret Pache ◆ Mesa, AZ

2 tablespoons butter
1 large onion, chopped
½ cup thinly sliced celery
½ red bell pepper, diced
2 cloves garlic, minced
1 jar (about 16 ounces) medium-hot salsa
2 cups cubed cooked ham
1 cup uncooked long-grain rice
1 cup water
⅔ cup vegetable broth
3 teaspoons extra-hot horseradish
2 teaspoons honey
¼ to ½ teaspoon hot pepper sauce
1½ pounds shrimp, peeled and deveined
1 tablespoon chopped fresh mint

1. Preheat oven to 350°F.

2. Melt butter in 3-quart Dutch oven over medium heat. Add onion, celery, bell pepper and garlic. Cook about 2 minutes or until vegetables are tender.

3. Add all remaining ingredients except shrimp and mint. Bake, covered, about 40 minutes or until rice is almost tender.

4. Remove from oven; stir in shrimp and mint; return to oven and bake additional 10 to 15 minutes or until shrimp are opaque.

Makes 6 to 8 servings

VOLUME MEASUREMENTS (dry)

1/8 teaspoon = 0.5 mL
1/4 teaspoon = 1 mL
1/2 teaspoon = 2 mL
3/4 teaspoon = 4 mL
1 teaspoon = 5 mL
1 tablespoon = 15 mL
2 tablespoons = 30 mL
1/4 cup = 60 mL
1/3 cup = 75 mL
1/2 cup = 125 mL
2/3 cup = 150 mL
3/4 cup = 175 mL
1 cup = 250 mL
2 cups = 1 pint = 500 mL
3 cups = 750 mL
4 cups = 1 quart = 1 L

VOLUME MEASUREMENTS (fluid)

1 fluid ounce (2 tablespoons) = 30 mL
4 fluid ounces (1/2 cup) = 125 mL
8 fluid ounces (1 cup) = 250 mL
12 fluid ounces (1 1/2 cups) = 375 mL
16 fluid ounces (2 cups) = 500 mL

WEIGHTS (mass)

1/2 ounce = 15 g
1 ounce = 30 g
3 ounces = 90 g
4 ounces = 120 g
8 ounces = 225 g
10 ounces = 285 g
12 ounces = 360 g
16 ounces = 1 pound = 450 g

DIMENSIONS

1/16 inch = 2 mm
1/8 inch = 3 mm
1/4 inch = 6 mm
1/2 inch = 1.5 cm
3/4 inch = 2 cm
1 inch = 2.5 cm

OVEN TEMPERATURES

250°F = 120°C
275°F = 140°C
300°F = 150°C
325°F = 160°C
350°F = 180°C
375°F = 190°C
400°F = 200°C
425°F = 220°C
450°F = 230°C

BAKING PAN SIZES

Utensil	Size in Inches/Quarts	Metric Volume	Size in Centimeters
Baking or Cake Pan (square or rectangular)	8 × 8 × 2	2 L	20 × 20 × 5
	9 × 9 × 2	2.5 L	23 × 23 × 5
	12 × 8 × 2	3 L	30 × 20 × 5
	13 × 9 × 2	3.5 L	33 × 23 × 5
Loaf Pan	8 × 4 × 3	1.5 L	20 × 10 × 7
	9 × 5 × 3	2 L	23 × 13 × 7
Round Layer Cake Pan	8 × 1 1/2	1.2 L	20 × 4
	9 × 1 1/2	1.5 L	23 × 4
Pie Plate	8 × 1 1/4	750 mL	20 × 3
	9 × 1 1/4	1 L	23 × 3
Baking Dish or Casserole	1 quart	1 L	—
	1 1/2 quart	1.5 L	—
	2 quart	2 L	—